CAREERS IN THE
BUILDING TRADES

Working in
Green Construction

Careers in the Building Trades

A Growing Demand

 Apprenticeships

 Carpenter

 Construction & Building Inspector

 Electrician

Flooring Installer

Heating and Cooling Technician

 Masonry Worker

Plumber

 Roofer

Working in Green Construction

CAREERS IN THE
BUILDING TRADES

A GROWING DEMAND

Working in
Green Construction

Andrew Morkes

MASON CREST

Mason Crest
450 Parkway Drive, Suite D
Broomall, Pennsylvania 19008
(866) MCP-BOOK (toll-free)
www.masoncrest.com

First printing

9 8 7 6 5 4 3 2 1
ISBN (hardback) 978-1-4222-4120-2

ISBN (series) 978-1-4222-4110-3

ISBN (ebook) 978-1-4222-7690-7

Cataloging-in-Publication Data on file with the Library of Congress

NATIONAL HIGHLIGHTS

Developed and Produced by National Highlights Inc.
Proofreader: Mika Jin
Interior and cover design: Yolanda Van Cooten
Production: Michelle Luke

CONTENTS

KEY ICONS TO LOOK FOR:

Words to understand: These words with their easy-to-understand definitions will increase the reader's understanding of the text while building vocabulary skills.

Sidebars: This boxed material within the main text allows readers to build knowledge, gain insights, explore possibilities, and broaden their perspectives by weaving together additional information to provide realistic and holistic perspectives.

Educational Videos: Readers can view videos by scanning our QR codes, providing them with additional educational content to supplement the text. Examples include news coverage, moments in history, speeches, iconic sports moments and much more!

Text-dependent questions: These questions send the reader back to the text for more careful attention to the evidence presented there.

Research projects: Readers are pointed toward areas of further inquiry connected to each chapter. Suggestions are provided for projects that encourage deeper research and analysis.

Series glossary of key terms: This back-of-the-book glossary contains terminology used throughout this series. Words found here increase the reader's ability to read and comprehend higher-level books and articles in this field.

INTRODUCTION

Green Construction Trades: Great Careers, Good Money, and Other Rewards

Green construction is the planning, design, building, and operation of structures in an environmentally responsible manner. It is also known as *green building* and *sustainable construction*. Green construction stresses energy and water efficiency, the use of eco-friendly construction materials (when possible), indoor environmental quality, the recycling and/or re-use of old building materials, and the structure's overall effects on its site or the larger community.

Green construction techniques are used in every trade—from carpentry and masonry, to plumbing, electrical work, and roofing. In 2017, one-third of single-family and multi-family home builders said that green construction was a significant aspect of their building activity, according to a survey conducted by the National Association of Home Builders and Dodge Data & Analytics. By 2022, this percentage is expected to increase to half.

Although demand is strong for construction workers (especially those who have knowledge of green construction techniques), only 6 percent of students consider a career in the trades, according to ExploretheTrades.org. Why? Because many young people have misconceptions about the trades. They have been told that the trades are low-paying, lack job security, and other untruths. In fact, working in the trades is one of the best career choices you can make. The following paragraphs provide more information on why a career in the trades is a good idea.

Good pay. Contrary to public perception, skilled trades workers earn salaries that place them firmly in the middle class. Average yearly salaries for construction workers in the United States are $48,900, according to the U.S. Department of Labor. This salary is slightly higher than the average earnings for some careers that require a bachelor's or graduate degree—including recreational therapists, $48,190; child, family, and school social workers, $47,510; and mental health counselors, $46,050. Trades workers who become managers or who launch their own businesses can have earnings that range from $90,000 to $200,000.

Strong employment prospects. There are shortages of trades workers throughout the world, according to the human resource consulting firm ManpowerGroup. In fact, trades workers are the most in-demand occupational field in the Americas, Europe, the Middle East, and Africa. They ranked fourth in the Asia-Pacific region.

Provides a comfortable life without a bachelor's or graduate degree. For decades in the United States and other countries, there has been an emphasis on earning a college degree as the key to life success. But studies show that only 35 percent of future jobs in the United States will require a four-year degree or higher. With college tuition continuing to increase and the chances of landing a good job out of college decreasing, a growing number of people are entering apprenticeship programs to prepare for careers in the trades. And unlike college students, apprentices receive a salary while learning and they don't have to pay off loans after they complete their education. It's a good feeling to start your career without $50,000 to $200,000 in college loans.

Rewarding work environment and many career options. A career in the trades is fulfilling because you get to use both your hands and your head to solve problems and make the world a better place. Working in green construction is even more exciting because green builders are at the cutting-edge of new construction practices and technology. They also get to help people save energy and protect the environment.

Jobs can't be offshored. Trades careers involve hands-on work that requires the worker to be on-site to do his or her job. As a result, there is no chance that your position will be offshored to a foreign country. In an uncertain employment atmosphere, that's encouraging news.

Job opportunities are available throughout the United States and the world. There is a need for trades workers in small towns and big cities. If demand for their skills is not strong in their geographic area, they can move to other cities, states, or countries where demand is higher.

Are the Trades Right for Me?

Test your interest in green construction. How many of these statements do you agree with?

☐ **I care about protecting the environment.**

☐ **I am interested in learning more about energy efficiency and green construction practices.**

☐ **My favorite class in school is shop.**

☐ **I like to build and repair things.**

☐ **I like to use power and hand tools.**

☐ **I like projects that allow me to work with my hands and use my creativity.**

☐ **I enjoy observing work at construction sites.**

☐ **I like to watch home-repair shows on TV and the internet.**

☐ **I don't mind getting dirty when I work on a project.**

☐ **I am good at math.**

If many of the statements above describe you, then you should consider a career in green construction. But you don't need to select a specific career right now. Check out the jobs in this book to learn more about occupational paths in the green trades. Good luck with your career exploration!

■ *Installing solar systems on roofs is just one way of using renewable energy.*

Words to Understand

carbon dioxide: A colorless, odorless gas that is naturally present in the earth's atmosphere. It is an important part of plant growth on earth, but if too much is released because of the burning of fossil fuels such as coal and oil, it can cause global warming and major damage to the environment.

geothermal power: Energy that is created by harvesting heat that exists below the earth.

retrofit: To add a component or system to a building that it did not have when it was constructed.

solar energy: Energy that is produced by harvesting the heat and energy of the sun.

sustainability: In the construction industry, an emphasis on building practices that save energy or reduce energy output, that use building materials from renewable resources such as wood and stone that can also be recycled or reused, and that incorporate other environmentally-friendly practices.

CHAPTER 1

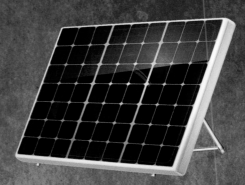

What Is Green Construction?

Do you care about protecting the environment? Are you interested in topics such as energy efficiency, recycling, sustainability, and solar energy? Do you like building things? If so, you might have a future in green construction.

Green construction is the process of planning, designing, building, and operating structures in an environmentally responsible manner. It is also known as *green building* and *sustainable construction*. Any type of building or structure—such as a home, factory, shopping center, hospital, or office building—can incorporate green construction features. A structure may be built from scratch using green construction practices, or an existing building may be retrofitted to use solar energy, an on-demand hot water pump (which reduces money spent on heating water), or energy-efficient lighting.

At first glance, a green building may not look all that different from a regular building. But if you walk around inside and on its roof, you'll see that green construction materials, building techniques, and components and systems have been used that allow the building's occupants to save money and energy, breathe healthier air, and otherwise enjoy the benefits of green construction.

■ *Installing a programmable thermostat allows users to monitor and reduce their energy usage.*

■ *Learn more about green building and the Leadership in Energy and Environmental Design green rating system:*

It's important to remember that not all green buildings are the same. There are many views of what makes a building green, and green construction practices and techniques vary around the world. With that said, here are some examples of features that many view as making a building "green":

■ *Daylighting allows more sunlight to enter a building, which reduces the need for electrical lighting and saves energy.*

The Benefits of Green Buildings

- Green buildings (new or renovated) are worth 7 percent more than non-green buildings.
- Researchers have discovered that better indoor air quality can lead to improvements of worker performance of up to 8 percent.
- Workers in green offices with good ventilation recorded a 101 percent increase in brain function.

Sources: Dodge Data & Analytics, Park and Yoon, Syracuse University Center of Excellence for Environmental and Energy Systems

- Consideration was made during the design process to create a building that is energy efficient and healthy for its occupants; that the structure will be resilient to events such as fires, flooding, and earthquakes; and that many of the building's rooms can be reused for a different purpose later (eliminating the need for costly and environmentally unfriendly remodeling)
- Building materials that are sustainable or recycled/reused, ethically produced, and nontoxic are used
- Efficient use of water, electricity, and other resources
- Effective use of natural lighting (sun roofs, etc.) to reduce energy costs
- Use of renewable energy such as solar and wind power
- Building systems that reduce and reuse waste water
- Good indoor air quality
- Use of renewable building materials (because some nonrenewable sources are becoming rarer and more expensive)
- Building systems and construction methods that reduce pollution and the destruction of the environment
- Landscaping that mimics the natural environment, rather than incorporating plants and trees that do not belong in an area and that require more watering; one example would be planting grass in the desert

- Wash clothes in cold water rather than hot
- Unplug rarely-used appliances
- Use your window shades to keep out the sun in the summer
- Install a programmable thermostat to control heating and cooling costs
- Turn off lights if you aren't using them
- Look for the Energy Star label, the U.S. government's symbol that the product is energy efficient; many other countries have a similar labelling process
- Change furnace/air-conditioner filters regularly; dirty filters = more energy use

Types of Green Building Techniques

The U.S. Department of Labor groups green building techniques into five categories. The following sections provide more information.

Location of the Structure

It might come as a surprise that planning for a new green building begins long before the first architectural sketch is drawn, but it's true. Careful plans must be made (especially when large buildings are being constructed) to ensure that the structure is as environmentally friendly and energy efficient as possible. *Urban planners* (experts who know how to organize cities and other areas for best use by their residents) and *architects* (skilled professionals who create the design of the entire building) carefully assess potential building sites to determine the best choice. For example, if a local government plans to build a new hospital, urban planners and architects study the potential sites to determine which is the most environmentally friendly. Following green building practices, they select the site that would have the least impact on the environment. For example, they might choose a site that is closer to or in a city to reduce the need for the building's eventual occupants to have to drive (which creates harmful exhaust that is bad for the environment). This would also reduce the need to build new roads and install water and plumbing pipes that would have to travel long distances to reach existing systems. Urban planners and architects might also seek to use preexisting structures to reduce building costs. Finally, the architect may decide to design and situate the building to take advantage of topography (the arrangement of the natural and human-made features in an area) or the building's shape that might save heating and cooling costs, or that allows for effective use of natural lighting.

Energy Efficiency

Buildings use a vast amount of energy—to light rooms and offices, to power heating and cooling systems, and for many other uses. In fact, the World Green Building Council reports that "buildings and construction together account for 36 percent of global final energy use and 39 percent of energy-related carbon dioxide emissions when upstream power generation is included." Green construction practices can significantly reduce energy use.

Some people might ask: what's so important about reducing energy? There are many reasons why cutting energy is a good idea, including:

- Saving money on heating, cooling, and lighting bills
- Reducing the amount of emissions from heating and cooling systems; these emissions damage the environment
- Reducing energy demand, which creates less need for governments to engage in sometimes harmful practices such as coal mining and oil and natural gas drilling
- Making your home or office more comfortable because there are fewer drafts
- You have to change fewer light bulbs

Architects, engineers, construction managers, and other trades workers use many different techniques to maximize energy efficiency. Owners of existing buildings can also take some of these steps to increase energy efficiency. Here are a few examples:

- Designing buildings to take advantage of natural lighting
- Installing daylighting in roofs, hallways, and other areas, which increases the admission of sunlight into a building to reduce electric lighting and save energy

■ *Using double-glazed glass prevents heat loss and saves energy.*

- Installing and servicing energy-saving furnaces and air-conditioners (including those that are full- or partly powered by solar energy, **geothermal power**, or other sources of green energy), programmable thermostats, and other energy-efficient equipment and devices

- Installing energy-saving appliances

- Installing light-emitting diode lighting (most people simply call these lights, LED lights) that produce light about 90 percent more efficiently than incandescent (traditional) light bulbs

- Using double-glazed glass to prevent heat loss

- In hot areas, using trees or shade from surrounding buildings to reduce the building's temperature

- Conducting energy audits of existing homes and businesses to help reduce the amount of energy being used and identify areas of the home or business where hot or cold air is being lost

- In some buildings, using renewable power sources to not only conserve energy, but also to produce it, which will reduce energy needs from outside sources

Water Conservation

Water covers more than 70 percent of the earth's surface, but most water contains salt and cannot be used unless the salt is removed via an expensive process. As a result, communities around the world are short of water. Many communities in desert areas already ration water (use water in only a specific allowed amount), while a few have run out of water entirely. Water shortages are a very serious issue—especially as the world's population grows, cities expand into areas that do not have large amounts of fresh water, aquifers (vast areas of underground water in permeable rock) become depleted (run out of water from overuse), and freshwater supplies are destroyed by pollution or by flooding from seawater during storms.

Green buildings seek to reduce the amount of water used and reuse water for other purposes after its first use. Water conservation strategies include:

- Installing devices that reduce the volume of water that is delivered by shower heads, faucets, and other plumbing hardware
- Installing low-flush toilets and/or those that have flush settings for solid waste and liquid
- Installing greywater recycling systems, water recovery systems that reuse greywater from showers, sinks, etc. for non-drinking purposes, such as for toilet flushing. Greywater is water that comes from showers, sinks, dishwashers, and washing machines that is relatively clean.
- Installing wireless technology that allows users to control water pressure and monitor water use
- Installing outdoor sprinkler systems that adjust the sprinklers accordingly over a certain time period based on weather forecasts. Sprinkler heads can also be set up to cover a specific area and have little or no overlap with other sprinkler heads to reduce water waste.
- Installing systems that collect rainwater that can be used to water plants and for other non-drinking purposes
- In existing buildings, conducting water audits of homes and businesses to help reduce the amount of water being used

■ *A rain barrel is used to collect rainwater runoff. The water from these water collection devices can be used to water plants and for other non-drinking purposes.*

■ *Learn how green construction techniques have been implemented at the National Renewable Energy Laboratory's Research Support Facility to save energy and money:*

Indoor Air Quality

We sometimes take air quality for granted. Some people reason that we have massive forests and lots of plants, which filter the air. On the other hand, we have tons of factories and vehicles emitting harmful smoke and exhaust, and plants and trees can't keep up. Air quality is poor in some U.S. cities and in many foreign countries. In fact, 92 percent of the world's population lives in places where air pollution exceeds safe limits, according to research from the World Health Organization.

This makes it even more important that the air inside our buildings is healthy to breathe. Types of indoor air pollution, include:

- Outdoor pollutants that are brought into the building
- Tobacco and other types of smoke
- Allergens such as pollen, dust, mold, and pet dander that are recognized by the immune system and cause an allergic reaction
- Household chemicals
- Chemical fumes from flooring, carpeting, paint, floor sealants, and other building materials
- Any other airborne substance that is introduced into the indoor environment that causes a negative effect on a building's occupants

■ *Ninety-two percent of the world's population lives in places where air pollution exceeds safe limits.*

Green building contractors, construction managers, and trades workers take the following steps to reduce or eliminate these issues:

- Use paints, finishes, and sealants that are less harmful to humans

- Use fiberglass, cellulose, or mineral wool to insulate buildings instead of more harmful materials such as asbestos

- Install quality air-conditioning and heating systems to ensure that clean air is provided

- Install air purification systems in buildings in areas with high outdoor pollution levels

Onsite Practices

One of the major ways to create a green building is to use green building materials and/or a combination of green materials and non-green materials that have been recycled from an existing building. Here are some ways in which construction managers and contractors use green building practices on-site during new construction or renovation projects:

- Before starting a project, choosing to work with companies that follow environmentally friendly building practices, such as using only sustainable wood or products that have been manufactured using green manufacturing processes

- Using bamboo, cork, medium-density fiberboard, or other products instead of traditional wood

- Reusing wood (reclaimed lumber), bricks, household fixtures, concrete (which can be used as gravel), and other building materials from existing structures that have been torn down

■ *Bamboo is just one type of renewable wood that has become popular in the green construction industry.*

- Using building supplies from local providers to reduce the burning of fossil fuels by trucks, ships, and trains that travel over long distances
- Recycling shingles, bricks, and other building supplies during renovation projects

Text-Dependent Questions

1. What is green construction?

2. What are three ways to improve energy efficiency in the home?

3. What are greywater recycling systems?

Research Project

Read the list of energy-saving tips in this chapter and check out the following website, https://blog.constellation.com/2016/01/01/31-ways-to-save-energy-in-your-home. Now, go through your home and identify what energy-efficiency tips you are following, and which you still need to do. Make a to-do list and work with your parents to make your home more energy efficient.

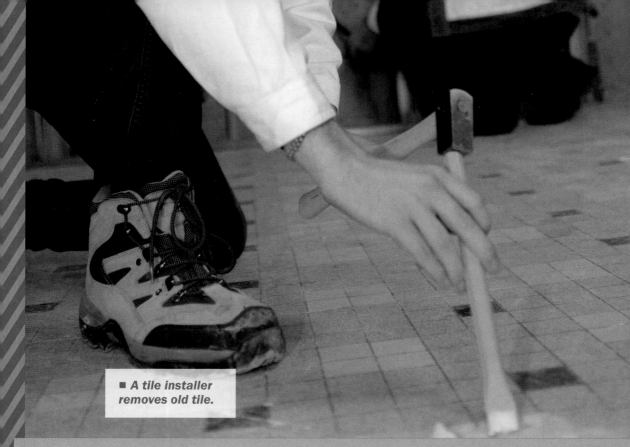

Words to Understand

blueprint: A reproduction of a technical plan for the construction of a home or other structure. Blueprints are created by licensed architects.

budget: A financial plan that details the amount of money that is available to spend on a project and its various components.

carbon footprint: The amount of greenhouse gas (carbon dioxide, methane, ozone, etc.) emissions created by a person, product, organization, building, or event. Greenhouse gases warm the earth's atmosphere.

oriented strand board: A popular type of structural, engineered wood panel that can be used for many purposes. It is manufactured using waterproof adhesives and rectangularly shaped wood strands.

photovoltaic: A type of technology that is used to generate electricity directly from sunlight via an electronic process.

CHAPTER 2

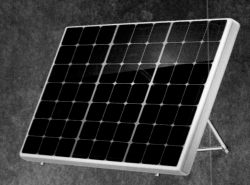

Careers in Green Construction

There are dozens, if not hundreds, of careers in the construction industry. Many of these occupations have a "green" element, in which the worker has been trained to use environmentally-friendly building materials and to install systems (heating, cooling, etc.) that help people save money, reduce energy waste, and live healthier lives. The following sections provide more information on careers in green construction:

Carpenters

There are two basic types of *carpenters: rough carpenters* and *finish carpenters*. Rough carpenters construct the inner frameworks of building and temporary structures (scaffolds, forms into which concrete is poured, bridge or sewer supports, etc.) by following blueprints or oral instructions from foremen and construction managers. They help build or repair homes, apartment buildings, factories, bridges, roads, railroads, airports, and any other structures. Rough carpenters are also known as *structural carpenters. Finish carpenters*, who are also known as *detail carpenters*, build and install cabinets, shelves, stairs, and floors that are made of wood, wood substitutes, and other materials.

■ *A construction manager (right) reviews blueprints with an apprentice.*

Here are some ways in which carpenters use green construction techniques and materials:

- Use reclaimed lumber or alternate (non-wood) building materials
- Use wood that has been certified as sustainable by the Forest Stewardship Council
- Use advanced framing techniques that require less wood and increase energy efficiency
- Use optimum value engineering principles, such as increasing the amount of spacing between framing pieces to use less lumber; this technique also increases energy efficiency because more insulation can be added
- Use structural insulated panels when building exterior walls for a new home or addition; these panels have a rigid foam that is situated between oriented strand board (which is manufactured from sustainable wood)
- Use engineered lumber that is made from what was once considered waste at the lumber mill (a place where wood is cut and prepared for sale)
- Reuse any existing building materials that can be safely repurposed in renovation projects
- Recycle or reuse any building materials that remain at the end of a project
- Install building components that can support wind turbines or solar cells.

Construction and Building Inspectors

Construction inspectors examine buildings and other structures to ensure that they have been built correctly. *Building inspectors* examine homes, condominiums, townhomes, and other new or previously owned buildings. They are also known as *home inspectors*. Some inspectors acquire specialized knowledge of green construction materials, techniques, and systems (heating, cooling, rainwater harvesting, refrigeration, water and air purification, etc.). Others develop expertise in renewable energy systems such as solar water heaters, windmills that generate the electricity to power homes and other buildings, and geothermal heating systems. Having such skills provides more job opportunities and higher earnings.

Construction Managers

Construction managers supervise every part of a construction project—from the various types of trades workers (carpenters, plumbers, steelworkers, etc. that do the actual work), to ordering supplies and equipment, to managing **budgets**, to ensuring that the job site is safe for workers. They play a major role in setting the tone of a green construction project. Some of their duties include:

- Ensuring that on-site processes are environmentally friendly
- Hiring trades workers with expertise in green construction practices
- Using sustainable and environmentally-friendly construction materials
- Setting up recycling plans for unused building materials
- Protecting environmentally sensitive areas (such as wetlands) at the work site.

Electricians

Electricians install, maintain, and repair electrical and power systems in homes and businesses. *Green electricians* do the following:

◄ *A technician installs solar panels.*

Architects plan and design houses, factories, skyscrapers, and other buildings and structures. Every major green construction project starts with architects, who make the key decisions (in cooperation with the builder or homeowner) about the use of sustainable building material, renewable energy sources, and the siting of structures so that they take advantage of natural lighting and have no (or a minimum) negative impact on the surrounding environment.

Plasterers apply plaster to ceilings, interior walls, and other areas of buildings, as well as to wire, wood, or metal. **Green plasterers** use clay plaster, that is completely non-toxic and environmentally friendly.

Solar photovoltaic installers build, install, and maintain solar panel systems. Some connect the solar arrays to the electric grid. Others install photovoltaic systems on the roofs of homes, businesses, and other buildings to provide renewable energy.

Wind turbine technicians install, maintain, and fix wind turbines, including their electrical, mechanical, and hydraulic components and systems. Some may install small turbines on large buildings to provide alternative, renewable energy.

Energy auditors conduct energy audits of buildings, process systems, and building systems to help building owners identify areas where energy is being wasted. They suggest improvements that will reduce energy waste and costs.

Weatherization installers and technicians install additional insulation, repair windows, insulate ducts, perform heating, ventilating, and air-conditioning work, and do other weatherization-related tasks to improve the energy efficiency of homes and other structures. Some also perform energy audits.

Insulation installers apply insulating materials (eco-friendly ones, if possible) to pipes and ductwork, in walls and ceilings, and under floors to reduce energy loss, which saves building owners money and stops the waste of heat or air-conditioning.

Painters apply paint, stains, and other coatings to walls, ceilings, buildings, and other structures. They use low– or zero–volatile organic compound adhesives to reduce or eliminate the creation of ozone (which causes global warming) and to create healthy indoor air.

Glaziers install glass in windows, skylights, and other places. To increase energy efficiency, glaziers install double-paned windows, which lose less interior heat than single-paned windows do. They also make sure that new or existing windows and skylights are properly installed and sealed so that unwanted hot or cold air from outside cannot get into a building.

- Install smart energy meters that track the use of electricity and that allow building owners to monitor and reduce their energy use
- Encourage building owners to install **photovoltaic** roofing shingles to fully or partly power a building
- Recommend other alternative energy sources such as wind and geothermal power, when appropriate
- Recommend the use of smart power strips, which stop plugged-in electronic devices from using unnecessary energy
- Encourage customers to install light-emitting diode bulbs, energy-efficient light bulbs that produce light that is about 90 percent more efficient than incandescent (traditional) light bulbs.

■ *Follow a day in the life of a solar installer:*

Flooring Installers

Flooring installers build and repair floors of all types. These include those made of hardwood, wood laminate, carpeting, stone, cork, vinyl, and other materials. Some flooring installers specialize in installing a certain type of flooring (such as carpeting), while others install many types of flooring. Green construction practices of flooring installers include:

- Using sustainable or engineered wood instead of less-environmentally friendly flooring materials
- Educating consumers about the eco-friendliest types of flooring

- Using low– or zero–volatile organic compound adhesives to reduce or eliminate the creation of ozone, which can create smog in the lower atmosphere and cause respiratory (breathing) problems
- Recycling existing flooring materials, when possible.

Heating and Cooling Technicians

Some *heating and cooling technicians* install and service residential heating, ventilation, and air-conditioning systems, while others work in commercial and industrial settings. Others install and repair air purification systems that protect us from allergens, household chemicals, and other pollutants. *Green heating and cooling technicians* perform job duties such as:

- Conducting energy audits of homes and businesses to help reduce the amount of energy being used and identify areas of the home or business where hot or cold air is being lost

■ *An insulation worker installs thermal insulation under a roof.*

- Six percent of the average household budget is spent on space cooling.

- Two-thirds of U.S. homes have air-conditioners.

- Homeowners can cut their air-conditioning energy use by 20 to 50 percent by purchasing a high-efficiency air-conditioner and embracing other green practices.

Source: U.S. Department of Energy

- Installing and servicing energy-saving furnaces and air-conditioners (including those that are fully- or partly powered by solar energy, geothermal power, or other sources of green energy)

- Installing programmable thermostats and other energy-efficient equipment and devices.

■ *Learn more about how masonry is used in sustainable building:*

Masonry Workers

Masonry workers, who are sometimes known as *masons*, use brick, tile, cement, stone (marble, granite, limestone, etc.), and other materials to create surfaces and structures such as walls, fences, fireplaces, bridges, roads, sidewalks, chimneys and high-temperature furnaces, and other structures. Many masonry building materials are sustainable and reusable, including bricks, stone, and tile. They also last a long time and require less maintenance than other building materials. The use of masonry materials (instead of other building materials) has been proven to reduce the buildup of mold and fungus between interior and exterior walls. They also provide excellent soundproofing. Masons practice green masonry by:

- Reusing building materials, when possible
- Using low- or zero-volatile organic compound adhesives to reduce or eliminate the creation of ozone
- Recycling or repurposing unused or damaged building materials.

Plumbers

There are two main types of *plumbers*—residential and commercial—and several types of specialists. *Residential plumbers* are the type of plumbers that you're probably most familiar with. They come to your house when your sink gets clogged or a pipe freezes. They install and repair pipes that carry liquids or gases to, from, and within our homes and other buildings. *Commercial plumbers* work on large plumbing systems at schools, hospitals, shopping centers, water parks, and sports stadiums. These buildings feature complex, industrial-grade pipes and fixtures.

Pipefitters install high-pressure and low-pressure pipe systems that carry gases, chemicals, and acids. They usually work in commercial, manufacturing, and industrial settings. Pipefitters can further specialize, working as *sprinkler fitters*, who install, maintain, and repair automatic fire sprinkler systems; *gasfitters*, who install and repair pipes that provide natural gas to cooling and heating systems and to stoves, as well as pipes that transport natural gas or those that provide oxygen to patients in hospitals; and *steamfitters*, who install and repair pipe systems that move

■ *An energy auditor inspects a water heater as part of an energy audit.*

steam under high pressure. *Pipelayers* install and repair pipes for sewer and drainage systems and oil and gas lines. These pipes are constructed out of iron, clay, concrete, and plastic.

Green plumbers have job duties such as:

- Helping residential customers or commercial contractors reduce water usage, recycle water, and make use of sustainable resources via the use of water-saving technologies, solar power for hot water, and installing hybrid water heaters that provide hot water on demand, and that have a low **carbon footprint**

- Conducting water audits of homes and businesses to help reduce the amount of water being used

- Insulating hot water pipes—especially those that are located by exterior walls—to reduce energy loss

- Installing and servicing water-saving devices (low-flow shower heads, toilets, etc.), the piping systems that attach to solar power systems, in-demand hot water pumps, and other related hardware and systems

- Installing a home leak-monitoring device to help homeowners quickly discover leaks and reduce water waste.

Roofers

Roofers install new roofs and repair existing ones. Some roofers specialize in repairing or building roofs of business and commercial buildings, such as factories,

Eight Ways to Lower Cooling Costs

1. Install a programmable thermostat
2. Use ceiling fans
3. Insulate walls and the attic
4. Seal cracks that allow heat to come into the home
5. Purchase an ENERGY STAR air-conditioner
6. Install energy-efficient window coverings
7. Use the bathroom fan when showering or taking a bath—doing so helps remove heat and humidity from the home
8. Install a "cool roof" that reflects the rays of the sun and reduces heat absorption

sports stadiums, department stores, restaurants, and office buildings. Others focus on residential roof repair and construction. *Green roofers* perform job duties such as:

- Installing solar energy roofing systems that have energy-collecting photovoltaic panels built into roofing membranes, tiles, or shingles
- Attaching solar panels to existing roofs
- Installing modular plant- and soil-holding systems over existing roof membranes to create green roofs; these systems include protective membranes, drainage and aeration components, water retention and filtering layers, soil substrates, irrigation (watering) materials, and plants
- Installing "cool roofs" that reflect the rays of the sun, thereby reducing the absorption of heat
- Encouraging customers to install daylighting, which increases the admission of sunlight into a building to reduce electric lighting and save energy
- Suggesting the use of metal roofing instead of asphalt or tile roofing because it lasts longer and provides better protection than conventional roofing

- Using energy-efficient roof membranes
- Using low- or zero-volatile organic compound adhesives
- Recycling asphalt roofing shingles—along with other construction debris—instead of dumping them into land-fills (places where garbage is dumped).

■ *A roofer lays tile.*

Text-Dependent Questions

1. What is green construction?

2. What are three ways to improve energy efficiency in the home?

3. What are greywater recycling systems?

Research Project

Learn more about green construction by visiting https://www.bls.gov/green/construction, https://archive.epa.gov/greenbuilding, and https://new.usgbc.org. Write a report that summarizes the pros and cons of using green construction methods and present it to your class.

CHAPTER 3

Terms of the Trade

allergen: Any substance such as pollen, dust, mold, and pet dander that is recognized by the immune system and causes an allergic reaction.

blackwater: Wastewater that contains urine or fecal matter that is not appropriate for recycling in homes or businesses.

building codes: A series of rules established by local, state, regional, and national governments that ensure safe construction. The International Green Construction Code regulates the environmentally-friendly construction of new and existing commercial buildings.

carbon footprint: The amount of greenhouse gas (carbon dioxide, methane, ozone, etc.) emissions created by a person, product, organization, building, or event. Greenhouse gases warm the earth's atmosphere.

certified lumber: Wood that has been harvested from forests that have been certified by the Forest Stewardship Council (FSC) as sustainably managed. Today, more than 380 million acres of forest are FSC-certified, including more than 150 million acres in the United States and Canada.

daylighting: Design practices that seek to increase the admission of sunlight into a building to reduce electric lighting and save energy.

energy audit: The process of going through a home or other building to determine where energy is being wasted, and suggesting solutions (smart meters, more insulation, etc.) to improve energy efficiency.

ENERGY STAR®: A program created by the U.S. Environmental Protection Agency that aims to help consumers and businesses select energy-efficient products and technologies. Similar programs are available in other countries.

envelope: In construction, the parts of a building that divide the outdoors from the indoors. These include the foundation, exterior walls, exterior windows and doors, attic floor, and/or roof.

geothermal power: Energy that is created by harvesting heat that exists below the earth.

greywater: Water that comes from showers, sinks, dishwashers, and washing machines that is relatively clean.

greywater recycling system: A water recovery system that reuses greywater from showers, sinks, etc. for non-drinking purposes, such as for toilet flushing.

high-performance home (HPH): A home that is much more energy efficient than a traditional home. Components of an HPH include power from clean energy sources, such as solar photovoltaic electricity; an air-tight, well-insulated, thermal envelope; filtration systems that create excellent indoor air quality; and highly-efficient heating and cooling systems.

hydronic heating system: A heating system that uses hot water that is heated by a boiler. The boiler is fueled by solar energy or geothermal energy. The heat is piped through tubes that run under floorboards, along base boards, or through radiators.

insulation: Any building material that helps maintain a comfortable indoor temperature as compared to the outside temperatures—thus reducing the cost of heating or cooling a building.

Leadership in Energy and Environmental Design program: A voluntary building certification program that was developed by the U.S. Green Building Council. It recognizes highly efficient and sustainable structures. Similar programs are available in other countries.

light-emitting diode bulbs: Energy-efficient light bulbs that produce light that is about 90 percent more efficient than incandescent (traditional) light bulbs. Commonly known as **LED lights**.

local/regional building materials: Those that have been produced or harvested within a specific distance from the building site—typically 500 miles (805 kilometers) but less if the materials are produced locally. Using these materials reduces pollution caused by transportation over long distances and provides a financial boost to the local community.

native vegetation: Plant and tree species that originated in a particular region and ecosystem without the need for humans to maintain them.

net zero building: A building that produces at least as much energy as it uses.

organic compound adhesives: Components found in some adhesive and sealant products that react with nitrogen oxides in the air and sunlight to create a gas called ozone, which can create smog in the lower atmosphere and cause respiratory problems.

permeable pavement: A paved surface that is constructed out of building material that allows for rain and other water runoff to soak into the ground. This type of pavement reduces the risk of flooding and allows water to return to the ecosystem.

photovoltaic: A type of technology that is used to generate electricity directly from sunlight via an electronic process.

pollutant: Any substance (such as tobacco and other types of smoke, household chemicals, etc.) that is introduced into the environment that causes a negative effect on humans, plants, animals, ecosystems, and the overall environment.

private water meter: A device installed in a home or other building that measures water flow. It allows the building's occupants to more accurately assess their water usage and adjust it to reduce water waste.

programmable thermostat: A device that can be used to set the desired temperature in a home or other building for a period of time [e.g., 64 degrees Fahrenheit (17 degrees Celsius) while a family sleeps, and 70 degrees Fahrenheit (21 degrees Celsius) during daytime hours]. It helps users save energy.

rainwater harvesting: The process of capturing and storing rain for future use, thereby reducing the amount of water used from other sources.

renewable energy: Sources of energy—such as solar, wind, hydropower, geothermal, and wave and tidal systems—that never run out.

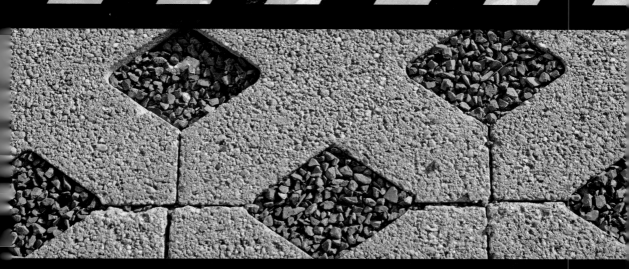

resilient home: A home that has the ability to maintain a comfortable environment even when a natural disaster, a dangerous weather event, or extended utility service interruption occurs. These homes have systems that generate their own power, reuse water, dispose of waste, and perform other tasks that are normally done by outside systems.

smart home technology: Electronic systems that automatically control and monitor lighting, heating, ventilation, and security systems, as well as appliances. They can be commanded by voice, remote control, tablet, or smartphone.

solar energy: Energy that is produced by harvesting the heat and energy of the sun.

solar module: An energy-efficient component that is placed on a roof to collect the sun's energy to heat or cool a building.

sustainability: In the construction industry, an emphasis on building practices that save energy or reduce energy output, that use building materials from renewable resources such as wood and stone that can also be recycled or reused, and that incorporate other environmentally-friendly practices.

xeriscaping: Landscaping (plants, trees, grass, etc.) that does not require routine irrigation (watering).

zero energy ready home: A term and certification program that is used by the U.S. Department of Energy. Refers to newly built homes or those that have been completely remodeled that are so energy efficient that their entire energy needs could be provided by renewable energy.

■ *High school students receive woodworking training in shop class.*

Words to Understand

fluent: The ability to speak or write a language other than your own native language.

fringe benefits: A payment or non-financial benefit that is given to a worker in addition to salary. These consist of cash bonuses for good work, paid vacations and sick days, and health and life insurance.

internship: A paid or unpaid learning opportunity in which a student works at a company or other employer to obtain experience. Internships can last anywhere from a few weeks to a year.

pension: A regular payment made to a retired person from a fund that the person and/or their employer has contributed to during the time they worked at the employer.

Registered Apprenticeship: An apprenticeship programs that meets standards of fairness, safety, and training established by the U.S. government or local governments.

CHAPTER 4

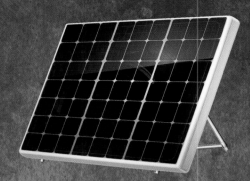

Preparing for the Field and Making a Living

Educational Paths

There are many ways to prepare for a career in construction and learn more about green building techniques and construction materials in the process. You can participate in an apprenticeship (the most popular entry method for most construction careers), attend a technical school or community college, learn through informal methods such as working as a helper to an experienced construction worker or by signing up for a program offered by a contractor, or receive training in the military. The following sections provide more information on recommended high school classes and educational paths.

High School Classes

Your high school years are a great time to begin building your construction skills, environmental knowledge, and other useful topics. Shop class is the most important course to take in high school. In it, you'll learn how to use hammers, drills, saws, and other tools. You'll learn how to repair and troubleshoot things. You'll learn how to build wood dressers and tables, metal toolboxes and lamps, and many other objects. Some will look great, and others—not so much. All trades workers learn by making mistakes, so shop training is very valuable. In some classes, you might even learn to weld or build a mini house with wood or carpeted floors and working water, electricity, heating, and air-conditioning.

Some shop programs may offer classes or lessons on green construction. If not, you could ask your shop teacher to cover this topic.

Environmental science classes will provide you with the big picture of how our actions positively and negatively affect the environment. They also teach the science behind global warming and global climate change.

Construction workers use math every day on the job, so be sure to take math classes, including basic algebra and trigonometry. For example, construction workers must know how to add, subtract, multiply, divide, and compute fractions and percentages to calculate various things (such as the number of bricks or shingles needed for a certain area, the proper mix of sand and cement, etc.) as they work. Electricians need to calculate various things like voltage drop, conduit shrinkage, and bending angles.

Philosophy classes will teach you to develop your critical-thinking skills. You'll be surprised how often you'll need to carefully think through a problem on the job.

If you plan to start your own company, you should take marketing, English/writing, accounting classes, and business classes. Additionally, computer science classes will come in handy because apprentices and other trainees use laptop computers, smart-boards, and other technology to learn. And trades workers use tablet computers to read blueprints at job sites and digital devices of all kinds (such as moisture meters, thermal imaging scanners, and laser levels) to do their jobs.

Foreign language classes will come in handy if you work in areas where many people do not speak the main language(s) of your country. For example, there are many Spanish-speaking construction workers in the United States. Some are **fluent** in English, while others may speak only a little English or not speak English at all. If you know Spanish, you'll be able to communicate with these people.

Other recommended courses include chemistry, blueprint reading, current events, and physics.

■ *Green construction workers often work with team members from other countries, so learning a foreign language will be useful.*

■ *Learn about a green construction training program:*

Pre-Apprenticeships

Some aspiring construction workers participate in pre-apprenticeship programs before entering an apprenticeship program. This allows them to learn more about the construction industry and specific careers before taking the big leap and applying to an apprenticeship program. Professional associations, community colleges, and unions offer pre-apprenticeship programs. Program lengths vary by country. In the United States, for example, pre-apprenticeship programs last anywhere from six to twelve weeks. On the other hand, a masonry pre-apprenticeship program offered by the Ontario Masonry Training Centre in Canada lasts thirty-two to forty weeks.

In the United States, Associated Builders and Contractors offers a pre-apprenticeship program that prepares students to enter a Registered Apprenticeship program. Some of the modules completed by participants include:

- Introduction to Construction Math
- Introduction to Hand Tools
- Introduction to Power Tools
- Introduction to Construction Drawings
- Introduction to Material Handling

The National Association of Home Builders offers pre-apprenticeship certificate training through its Home Builders Institute. (A certificate is a credential that shows

The Benefits of Pre-Apprenticeship Programs

The U.S. Department of Labor says that there are many benefits to participating in a pre-apprenticeship program, including:

- Allows you to investigate and learn about career options
- Allows you to receive classroom- and technology-based training
- Builds your math, English, literacy, and work-readiness skills that employers want in apprentices and employees
- Prepares you to advance into a Registered Apprenticeship program.

that a person has completed specialized education, passed a test, and met other requirements to qualify for work in a career or industry.) The program is geared toward high school and college students, transitioning military members, veterans, justice-involved youth and adults, and unemployed and displaced workers. Programs are available in the following areas: Masonry, Plumbing, Carpentry, Building Construction Technology, Weatherization, Electrical, Landscaping, and Painting.

Apprenticeships

The majority of construction workers prepare for the field by completing an apprenticeship program, which, in the United States, typically lasts three to five years, although some programs are shorter. During each year in the program, trainees complete 2,000 hours of on-the-job training and 144 hours of related classroom instruction. Entry requirements vary by program, but typical requirements include:

- Minimum age of eighteen (in Canada and some other countries, the minimum age is sixteen)

■ *An electrical instructor offers tips to an apprentice (left).*

- High school education
- One year of high school algebra
- Qualifying score on an aptitude test
- Drug free (illegal drugs)

Visit www.doleta.gov/OA/sainformation.cfm for information on apprenticeship training programs in your state. If you live in another country, contact your country's department of labor.

In Canada and other countries, aspiring construction workers in some fields can enter high school apprenticeship programs that prepare them for work. Visit https://www.canada.ca/en/employment-social-development/services/apprentices.html for more information on apprenticeship programs in Canada.

As they progress through the program, apprentices learn more skills, are given more responsibility, and receive higher wages. Those who complete an apprenticeship training program are known as journeymen.

Technical and Community College

Some construction workers train for their field by earning a certificate, diploma, and/or an associate degree in a specific trade (e.g., carpentry, masonry, heating/cooling, etc.) or one in construction management or general construction from a technical college or community college. A technical college is a public or private college that offers two- or four-year programs in practical subjects, such as the trades, applied sciences, and engineering. A community college is a public or private two-year school that awards certificates and associate degrees, and sometimes bachelor's degrees. In college programs, you'll learn via classes and hands-on training via workshops and internships. Some college programs have relationships with formal apprenticeship programs.

A few colleges offer certificates and degrees in green construction or green technology (solar power, wind energy, geothermal power, etc.). Typical classes in a green construction associate degree program include: Construction Math, Interior and Exterior Finishes, Electrical and Mechanical Systems, Quantity and Cost Estimating, Administration and Scheduling, Introduction to Computer-Aided Design, Green Professional, Solar Energy Technology, Building Energy Codes, Design and Planning, and Fundamentals of Public Speaking.

Informal Training Opportunities

Another way to train for the field is by working as a helper to an experienced trades worker for three to five years. At first, you'll be assigned basic tasks. For example, mason helpers might be tasked with setting up work sites and mixing mortar, while a heating and cooling technician helper will be asked to fetch tools and supplies, clean furnaces, and insulate refrigerant lines. Gradually, you'll be trusted with more complicated tasks, such as laying tile or installing pipes for air-conditioning systems. While you're working as a helper, it's a good idea to take some college construction classes in your specialty, take some green construction classes, or even earn a certificate or diploma to expand your skills and knowledge.

Other Training Opportunities

Some large contractors operate their own training programs. These are not recognized apprenticeship programs, but they offer similar classroom and on-the-job instruction. Contact contractors in your area about potential training opportunities.

Military

Militaries around the world need construction workers to build and repair buildings, bridges, dams, bunkers, and other structures; install and repair electrical wiring systems; install pipe systems for water, steam, gas and waste; and perform many other duties. The U.S. military provides training in the following construction specialties: boilermakers, civil engineers, cement masons and concrete finishers, civil engineering technicians, construction carpenters, construction equipment operators, earth drillers, electricians, paving and related equipment operators, pipe fitters and steamfitters, plumbers, rock splitters, surveying technicians, and surveyors.

Visit TodaysMilitary.com for more information on opportunities with the U.S. military. It's important to remember that the military provides general construction

■ *Military masons build a wall.*

44

Construction Career Path

If you work hard and develop your construction skills, there are good opportunities for advancement. Here is a typical career ladder for green construction workers.

Green Construction Consultant: Has expertise in green building materials, construction techniques, green building certifications, and energy-efficient furnaces, air conditioners, and other systems.

Business Owner: Operates a contracting firm that provides services to homeowners and businesses. Typically licensed to offer specialized construction services.

Project Manager: Oversees entire projects, including staffing, ordering supplies and equipment, quality control, and other tasks.

Foreman: A journeyman who manages a group of other journeymen and apprentices on a project.

Journeyman: Has completed apprenticeship training. If licensed, can work by him- or herself without direct supervision, but, for large projects, must work under permits issued to a contractor.

Apprentice: In the United States, apprentices complete 2,000 hours of on-the-job training and 144 hours of related classroom instruction during each year of a three- to five-year course of study.

training, but not training in green building techniques, unless, like energy efficiency measures, they clearly save energy and money. If you train via the military, you'll also need to take green construction classes at a community or technical college.

How Much Can I Earn?

There is not much information available about salaries for green construction workers. Few construction workers focus on green construction practices full time. Most use green construction practices as part of their regular duties.

But there is a lot of salary information for construction workers. And recent news stories show that a college degree is not the only ticket to a well-paying, stable career.

Which Educational Path is Best for Me?

Apprenticeship

Pros: The most popular training path for aspiring construction workers because it provides a clear path to employment. You get paid while you learn (unlike college), and your earnings increase as you gain experience.

Cons: Programs typically last three to five years.

A Good Fit: For those who like a structured environment that combines both classroom and hands-on training.

Technical School/Community College

Pros: Programs last only one to two years.

Cons: You must pay tuition and you do not get paid like apprentices do (unless your program is affiliated with an apprenticeship program).

A Good Fit: For those who want to enter the workforce more quickly.

Informal Training

Pros: Allows you to get to work right away and receive a salary.

Cons: Training often not as detailed as apprenticeship or college.

A Good Fit: For those who do not need a structured educational setting to learn and who are able to pick up their skills and knowledge on the job.

Military Training

Pros: You receive quality training and a salary, and possibly get to travel the world.

Cons: You'll be required to serve your country for two or more years anyplace in the world, including in a war zone.

A Good Fit: For those who respect authority, and have a disciplined personality.

Research conducted by government agencies and professional associations shows that skilled trades workers such as carpenters, electricians, and masons can earn incomes that are comparable, and sometimes even higher, than those with college degrees.

In the United States, construction workers earn average salaries of $48,900, which is only slightly less than the average ($49,630) for all careers in America. Workers in some construction careers earn higher salaries than the national average. These

■ *In the United States, architects earn average salaries of nearly $82,000 a year.*

include elevator installers and repairers ($76,860), construction and building inspectors ($61,250), and plumbers, pipefitters, and steamfitters ($56,030).

Top Earners

The highest-paid construction workers who don't own a business can earn $75,000 or more, according to the USDL. Who earns this type of money? The most highly-skilled and experienced workers, those who supervise or manage others (but aren't business owners), and those who live in large cities and other areas with high demand for certain construction specialties and a shortage of workers. Contractors with successful businesses can earn $90,000 to $200,000 or more, depending on the size of their companies.

Union members often receive medical insurance, a **pension**, and other benefits from their union. Self-employed workers must provide their own **fringe benefits**.

Average Salaries for Trades Workers in the United States

- Construction Managers: $99,510
- Architects: $81,920
- Construction and Building Inspectors: $61,250
- Electricians: $56,650
- Plumbers, Pipefitters, and Steamfitters: $56,030
- Wind Turbine Service Technicians: $54,360
- Brickmasons and Blockmasons: $53,440
- Carpenters: $48,340
- Heating and Cooling Technicians: $48,320
- Glaziers: $47,260
- Tile and Marble Setters: $44,770
- Plasterers and Stucco Masons: $44,070
- Carpet, Floor, and Tile Installers and Finishers: $43,950
- Pipelayers: $42,860
- Solar Photovoltaic Installers: $42,500
- Roofers: $42,080
- Painters and Paperhangers: $41,430

Earnings for Apprentices

Many people pursue training via an apprenticeship because of the quality education it offers and because they actually get paid a salary while they learn. Who doesn't like to earn while they earn? This is especially true because the average U.S. college undergraduate has $37,172 in student loan debt, according to The Institute for College Access & Success.

Apprentices typically begin by earning between 40 percent and 50 percent of what trained trades workers make. They receive pay increases as they gain experience. By the end of their training, their salary matches that of an entry-level journeyman in their field.

Earnings for Helpers

Some people train to be construction workers by working as helpers to experienced trades workers. Construction trades helpers earn average salaries of $30,900. Here are the average salaries for various types of construction helpers, according to the USDL:

- Helpers-brickmasons, blockmasons, stonemasons, and tile and marble setters: $33,610
- Helpers-carpenters: $30,200
- Helpers-electricians: $30,980
- Helpers-painters, paperhangers, plasterers, and stucco masons: $28,760
- Helpers-pipelayers, plumbers, pipefitters, and steamfitters detail: $30,640
- Helpers-roofers: $28,890.

Text-Dependent Questions

1. What high school classes should you take to prepare for a career in green construction?

2. What is the most popular training method for aspiring construction workers, and what does it involve?

3. What are some of the highest-paying construction careers? The lowest-paying?

Research Project

Learn more about apprenticeships by visiting https://www.dol.gov/apprenticeship. Ask your school counselor or shop teacher to help set up an information interview with an apprentice or apprenticeship coordinator in your favorite construction field to get a better understanding of the apprenticeship process.

ON THE JOB
Interview with a Professional

Michael Trolle is a cofounder and principal of BPC Green Builders, Inc. (https://www.bpcgreenbuilders.com) in Wilton, Connecticut.

Q. Can you tell me about your business?

A. We build custom homes for people who hire us to manage the full process. Our focus is on the use of building science to achieve superior performance in terms of energy efficiency, indoor air quality, comfort, safety, and durability. Often, we incorporate details that address other concerns related to sustainability. We start by providing consulting and estimating services because few architects have the expertise to incorporate the necessary details on the plans and because any design is better if there's a collaboration between builder and architect. If the estimate is acceptable, we then sign a construction contract to manage all aspects of the construction, including purchase of all materials and selection and management of all subcontractors, leading to a finished house that is third-party certified to one or more of the green certification standards, such as EPA Energy Star for Homes, DOE Zero Energy Ready Homes, PHIUS Passive House, and USGBC LEED for Homes.

Q. What made you want to get into this field?

A. I got into the field because I had an interest in both sustainability and residential construction. My initial research led me to green building conferences, where I was introduced to building science. This was a huge eye-opener for me because I learned that the home building industry was stuck in the mud, utilizing decades-old concepts and strategies and convinced that homeowners would not pay anything extra up-front for the guts of a house if they couldn't see what they were getting in the finished product. Building science was about how wrong this thinking was and that highly energy-efficient homes could be built for a small premium with a quick cost return and with a perpetual return in terms of all of the desirable performance factors I listed earlier. I knew that I had found my passion and my calling once I was exposed to this information.

Q. What are the pros and cons of owning a green construction business?

A. The pros are that you are your own boss and can call the shots. It's both your vision and your responsibility to chart a path forward to realizing that vision. The cons include that you can't avoid the hard stuff, unless you're big enough to hire someone else to do it. Another con is that there is a constant temptation to work like a dog because you know it has to get done, and there's nobody else to do it. Finally, you're going to be limited by your own ability to chart the best path forward, unless you're smart enough to know when to get advice, something I did well at times and not at other times when I was starting out.

Q. What personal traits are important for green trades workers?

A. I don't think that there is anything special related to green trades only. The best advice for any trade has always been to do something that you care about and for which you have a passion.

Q. What advice would you give to someone who is considering a career in green construction?

A. Get appropriate education and training. Many of the new building-science based strategies and materials have not been adopted yet in mainstream construction practice. You need to become a building science expert as quickly as possible. Much of your work will require traditional skills and practices, but it's likely that you will be integrating new practices into many of these tasks.

Q. Is green construction a growing field? If so, why?

A. Yes. Building-science–based green building is mostly common sense and cost effective over the long term, when you consider the life span of a well-built home. Moreover, it has been making its way into the building codes and standard practices for the last thirty years, and this will inevitably continue.

■ *Many construction workers, such as masons, must be able to lift heavy weights.*

Words to Understand

ethnic group: A collection of people who have a shared connection based on their homeland, cultural heritage, history, ancestry, language, or other factors.

invoicing: The process of preparing and sending a customer a bill for work that has been completed.

nonprofit organization: A group (unlike a corporation or other for-profit business) that uses any profits it generates to advance its stated goals (protecting the environment, helping the homeless, etc.).

soft skills: Personal skills that people need to develop to interact well with others and be successful on the job. They include communication, work ethic, teamwork, decision making, positivity, time management, flexibility, problem solving, critical thinking, conflict resolution, and other skills and traits.

CHAPTER 5

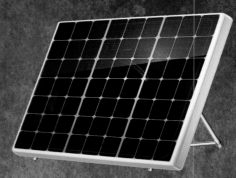

Key Skills and Methods of Exploration

What All Green Construction Workers Need

Green construction workers certainly need to be good with their hands, but they also need strong soft skills such as a talent for communication, problem solving, time management, and customer service. Here are some of the most important physical and soft skills for green construction workers:

- **Good dexterity, hand speed, and hand–eye coordination.** You'll need these skills to deftly place carpeting, tile, wood planks, shingles, roof tiles, bricks, or whatever building material that you're using. You'll need to work quickly (before adhesives harden) and accurately to keep jobs on schedule. Dexterity and good hand-eye coordination are also important when you're repairing electrical components, plumbing fixtures, air-conditioners, and other hardware.

■ *Roofers, carpenters, masons, and other construction workers often work at great heights, so good balance is important.*

- **Color vision.** This is especially important for certain careers. For example, electricians must be able to identify electrical wires by color. If you are unable to identify wiring by color, you could be electrocuted and be injured or even die. Good color vision is also important for tile installers, marble setters, and masons, who must be able to identify small color variations, as well as choose amongst the most attractive color combinations when installing these materials to create the best finished look.

- **Physical stamina and strength.** The life of a green construction worker involves constant movement. You'll spend a great deal of your day stooping, bending, reaching, and kneeling, as well as climbing ladders or scaffolds (so good balance is also important, as well as no fear of heights). Many careers in this field—such as carpenter, roofer, plumber, and mason—are physically demanding. For example, masons may have to carry bags of mortar and grout and equipment that can weigh more than fifty pounds (22.7 kilograms). Carpenters must carry plywood sheets that can weigh anywhere from fifty to one-hundred pounds (22.68 to 45.36 kilograms).

- **Artistic ability.** It might seem surprising that construction workers need to be artistic, but it's true. If you work as a mason, for example, you'll need a good sense of how different colors, patterns, and textures work together to create an attractive finished product.

- **Flexibility and problem-solving skills.** You'll encounter challenges every day on the job. For example, building materials may arrive late or not match project specifications. Blueprints may not match what you actually see on the job site. The ability to keep your cool and solve problems quickly will come in handy on the job.

- **Detail-oriented.** Attention to detail is the difference between a quality job and a poorly-done one. For example, if you fail to weld pipes together correctly, you could have a major refrigerant leak. If you forget to add the wood spacers when installing a wood floor, the flooring won't be able to expand and contract based on levels of humidity—and this could damage the floor. You won't be in business long if you fail to keep track of customer appointments and **invoicing**, order supplies, and do other tasks.

- **Green industry knowledge.** You'll need to be an expert in green construction building materials and techniques, energy efficiency strategies, and high-performance furnaces, air-conditioners, and other green products. This will require constant learning and the willingness to continue to update your knowledge because green building practices change all the time.

- **Enthusiasm.** You must not only be knowledgeable about green construction, but you need to be excited about all the cutting-edge ways you can help your customers save money, reduce energy waste, and live healthier lives. Customers like to work with contractors who are enthusiastic and excited about sustainable building.

- **Communication and persuasion skills.** These skills are extremely important in the green construction industry because, not only will you need to explain standard construction materials and practices, you'll also need to explain why customers should use green building materials, techniques, and products instead of traditional materials and products. For example, you'll need to be able to explain to customers why it's a good idea to replace their energy inefficient water heater with a solar-powered one. If you're a flooring installer, you'll need to be able to explain the differences in quality, durability, and price (as well as environmental impact) of installing wood or laminate flooring, or between carpeting and vinyl flooring.

- **Customer-service skills.**
Whether you own a business or you're the main customer-contact person for your company, you must be polite, courteous, friendly, and patient with customers. You should also have good listening skills. The construction industry is very competitive, and companies that don't offer good customer service won't last long.

- **Teamwork/interpersonal skills.**
If you work as a member of a team, you'll need to learn how to work with people from different backgrounds, ethnic groups, ages, and experience levels.

■ *Green construction workers must have excellent communication skills.*

Habitat for Humanity

Habitat for Humanity is a nonprofit housing organization that operates in nearly fourteen-hundred communities across the United States and in more than seventy countries around the world to build affordable housing and repair existing homes for those in need. Through its Youth Programs (https://www.habitat.org/volunteer/near-you/youth-programs), Habitat for Humanity offers volunteer opportunities for those age five to forty. High school and college students can start a Habitat chapter at their schools, volunteer to build or fix houses for a week during school breaks, and get involved in other ways that allow them to learn about home construction and make the world a better place.

■ *A Habitat for Humanity volunteer helps build a home.*

Exploring Green Construction as a Student

There are many ways as a middle school or high school student to learn more about green construction and careers in the field. Tours of green houses, classes, clubs, do-it-yourself activities, competitions, and information interviews are just a few ways to learn more. Here's a rundown of some popular methods of exploration:

■ *Take math classes in high school because green construction workers use their math skills every day on the job.*

Take Some Classes. There are a variety of classes that will help you to learn more about green construction and construction in general. Other classes will give you a good background should you decide to start your own green construction business. Here are some recommended classes: shop class, environmental science, earth science, geology, math (especially basic algebra and trigonometry), chemistry, physics, and foreign languages.

If you plan to start your own business, take business, marketing, English/writing, speech, computer science, and accounting.

Attend an Open House. Many college construction and apprenticeship programs host open houses to educate young people about their programs. At such an event, you'll tour classrooms and hands-on work areas and learn how to bend sheet metal, install electrical wiring, apply mortar to a trowel, and do other construction tasks. Contact schools and unions in your area to learn about upcoming open houses.

Build Something! It might seem overwhelming at first, but try to build a mini-wall using environmentally-friendly building materials. Do the same to build a table or a lamp. These projects will allow you to get your hands dirty, become familiar with tools, develop your critical-thinking skills, and learn more about green construction. These projects can also be a lot of fun, so start building! Ask your shop teacher to provide project ideas. YouTube is an excellent source of how-to videos.

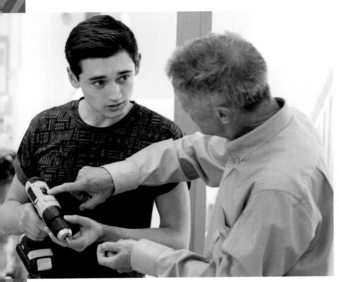

Try Out Some Tools. Hammers, levels, saws, chisels, and trowels are just a few of the many tools green construction workers use in their jobs. Now is the time to experiment with these and other tools so that you've at least had some experience when you start shop class or, eventually, begin an apprenticeship. You might find some of these tools in your parents' garage, at a hardware store, or at a local library (some have tool lending programs). Your shop teacher and parents can teach you how to use many of these tools (especially more dangerous power tools such as electric saws, nail guns, and power drills). YouTube is another good source for tips.

■ *A shop instructor teaches a student how to use a drill.*

COURTESY LUCY BRIGGS

Boulder High School student thinking small
LUCY BRIGGS BUILDS HER TINY DREAM HOUSE
NOW
NEWS

■ *A high school student builds a tiny house from the ground up:*

Join or Start a Construction Club at Your School. Your high school probably has a construction club, where you can learn how to use tools and build things, as well as learn about construction practices. Your faculty advisor may be able to set up presentations by green construction workers or tours of construction sites. If your school doesn't have one, work with your shop teacher to start one.

Guides for Aspiring Plumbers, Electricians, and Heating and Cooling Technicians

The Nexstar Legacy Foundation is a U.S.-based organization that seeks to attract young people to the heating, air-conditioning, plumbing, and electrical industries. It offers the Personal Guide Program to match those interested in these fields with a current heating and cooling technician, plumber, or electrician. If you participate in this program, you can ask the guide questions about his or her career, what they like and dislike about the field, potential career paths, and other topics. The guide can help you select a trade school, give you advice about apprenticeships, and help with scholarship applications. Visit http://explorethetrades.org/what-we-do/personal-guide-program to sign up for this free program.

Join the Technology Student Association. If you're a middle school or high school student and interested in science, technology, engineering, and mathematics (STEM), consider joining the Technology Student Association (TSA, http://www.tsaweb.org). This national, **nonprofit organization** offers sixty competitions at its annual conference, as well as opportunities to develop your leadership skills, perform community service, and compete for money for college. TSA is a good option for any aspiring green construction worker who is interested in electrical systems, energy efficiency, solar power, and related topics. Ask your school counselor or science teacher if your school has a TSA chapter and, if not, encourage them to start one.

Take a quiz. The Nexstar Legacy Foundation offers a 35-question quiz that assesses your interests, skills, workplace preferences, and technical knowledge to help you to determine if you would make a good heating and cooling technician, plumber, or electrician. At the end of the quiz, you're matched with a career and given more information about it. Visit http://explorethetrades.org/what-we-do/education/what-trade-is-right-for-you to take the quiz.

Participate in a Competition. Contests are a good way to build your skills and test your talents against those of your classmates or students from around the country or world. They are sponsored by schools, local park districts, or regional, national, or

Sources of Additional Exploration

Contact the following organizations for more information on education and careers in green construction:

Associated General Contractors of America
http://www.agc.org

Canada Green Building Council
https://www.cagbc.org

Green Building Council of Australia
https://new.gbca.org.au

Green Mechanical Council
https://www.escogroup.org/greenmech

Home Builders Institute
http://www.hbi.org

Irish Green Building Council
https://www.igbc.ie

National Association of Home Builders
https://www.nahb.org

National Center for Construction Education & Research
https://www.nccer.org

UK Green Building Council
https://www.ukgbc.org

U.S. Green Building Council
https://new.usgbc.org

World Green Building Council
http://www.worldgbc.org

international membership organizations for young people interested in construction, science, technology, engineering, math, and other fields. Here are some well-known organizations that host competitions that will allow you to develop and demonstrate your construction skills and knowledge. Although none focus specifically on green building skills, these competitions will help you to develop the basic skills that any trades worker needs.

■ *A teen performs a task during a bricklaying competition.*

- **SkillsUSA** (http://www.skillsusa.org) is a national membership organization for middle school, high school, and college/postsecondary students who are preparing for careers in trade, technical, and skilled service occupations. Its SkillsUSA Championships involve competitions in one hundred events, including Carpentry; Electrical Construction Wiring; Heating, Ventilation, Air Conditioning, and Refrigeration; Masonry; and Plumbing.

- **Skills Compétences Canada** (http://skillscompetencescanada.com/en/skills-canada-national-competition). This nonprofit organization seeks to encourage Canadian youth to pursue careers in the skilled trades and technology sectors. Its National Competition allows young people to participate in more than forty skilled trade and technology competitions, including Carpentry, Brick Masonry, and Workplace Safety.

- The **Technology Student Association** (http://www.tsaweb.org), a membership organization for middle and high school students interested in STEM, offers many competitions that allow students to demonstrate their skills. Examples include the Electrical Applications Competition for middle school students, and the Animatronics Competition for high school students. Other contests available for those with an interest in electricity and building things include TEAMS (Tests of Engineering Aptitude, Mathematics, and Science), a one-day competition for students in middle and high school; Junior Solar Sprint, an educational program for 5th through 8th graders; and the VEX Robotics Competition for middle and high school students.

Tour a Green Construction Site or Green Home. Touring a green construction site will allow you to see green builders on the job. You can ask them what type of green and energy-efficient building materials and practices they're using to build the structure, and you may even get a chance to use a hammer or learn how to use a mason's line. Ask your school counselor or shop teacher to arrange a tour of a green construction site. Some industry organizations (such as Go Construct in the United Kingdom) arrange tours to educate young people about construction specialties. Local construction associations and unions may also have information on tour opportunities.

Also consider taking a tour of a finished green home or other building. This is an excellent way to learn more about green construction and its benefits. For example, the Illinois Green Alliance (in the United States) offers the annual GreenBuilt Home Tour, a two-day program of tours of exceptional, award-winning, and nationally-recognized sustainable homes throughout Illinois. If you don't live in or near Illinois, check if tours are available in your area. You can also visit the alliance's website, http.//www.greenbuilthometour.org, to view photos, illustrations, and detailed descriptions of these green homes.

Participate in an Information Interview or Job Shadow a Green Construction Worker. In an information interview, you simply talk to a green construction worker about his or her job. Your goal is information, not a job like the "interview" part of "information interview" might suggest. Here are some questions to ask during the interview:

- Why did you want to specialize in green construction?
- Can you tell me about a day in your life on the job?
- What's your work environment like? Do you have to travel for your job?
- What are the most challenging tools to use?
- What are the most important personal and professional qualities for people in your career?

- What do you like best and least about your job?
- What do you do to keep yourself safe on the job?
- What is the future employment outlook in green construction?
- What can I do now to prepare for the field?
- What do you think is the best educational path to prepare for a career in green construction?

Job shadowing a green construction worker is another way to get a firsthand look at the world of sustainable building. In this type of learning experience, you follow a green roofer or a green mason around for a few hours or even an entire day on the job. You can observe them as they do their jobs, and ask them questions about specific tools, green building materials, energy efficiency, or other topics.

Professional associations, unions, shop teachers, career counselors, and friends and family who know green construction workers can help you arrange an information interview or job shadowing experience.

Text-Dependent Questions

1. What are some important skills for construction workers?

2. What is SkillsUSA and what does it offer to students?

3. What is an information interview? What questions should you ask during such an interview?

Research Project

Conduct research to learn more about green building materials and energy efficiency. Create a poster that summarizes your research and show it to your class.

■ *Employment for bricklayers in the United States is expected to grow faster than the average for all careers during the next decade.*

Words to Understand

Baby Boomer: A person who was born from the early-to-mid 1940s through 1964.

cost-effective: Doing something that is effective based on its cost. For example, walking a mile instead of driving, to save money. An example of an action that is not cost-effective would be paying your employees more than what you are being paid to do a job; you would make no money.

economy: Activities related to production, use, and trade of services and goods in a city, state, region, or country.

recruitment firm: A company that helps job-seekers find jobs, as well as assists employers who are seeking to fill open positions.

CHAPTER 6

The Future of Green Construction

The Big Picture

Skilled construction workers are in demand all over the world. Globally, workers in the skilled trades were cited by employers as the most in-demand career field, according to the human resource consulting firm ManpowerGroup. By continent or region, skilled trades workers topped the most in-demand list in the Americas, Europe, the Middle East, and Africa. They ranked fourth in the Asia-Pacific region.

Job opportunities for skilled construction workers in the United States are expected to be good. In fact, employment in the construction industry is expected to grow by 11 percent during the next decade, according to the U.S. Department of Labor (USDL), or 4 percent higher than the average growth for all industries. The USDL reports that "overall growth in the economy and population will increase demand for new buildings, roads, and other structures, which will create new jobs in construction and extraction occupations." There will be many new jobs for construction workers because of the following factors:

■ *In Canada, career opportunities will be especially strong for carpenters, construction machine operators, electricians, glaziers, plumbers, and roofers.*

- Many **Baby Boomer** installers are approaching retirement age, and there are currently not enough trainees to fill replacement needs.

- The U.S. population is growing, which is creating a residential building boom.

- Natural disasters such as earthquakes, floods, tornadoes, hurricanes, and massive wildfires will create demand for construction workers. For example, wildfires destroyed at least 8,400 homes and buildings in Northern California in the United States in October 2017. Construction workers from many fields were needed to help rebuild these homes.

■ *Learn why so many people are embracing green building:*

Strong Opportunities Expected in Green Construction

Green construction practices are being embraced around the world as a way to save money, reduce energy waste, increase the use of renewable building materials and renewable energy, and construct buildings that create better outdoor air, water, and soil quality, as well as do less damage to surrounding ecosystems. Consumers are also embracing green building because these construction practices create a healthier indoor environment (better air and water quality, etc.).

In 2016, 46 percent of U.S. construction firms said that they expected to work on new green institutional buildings during the next three years, compared to 38 percent of construction firms in other countries, according to the World Green Building Trends Study from Dodge Data & Analytics. Forty-three percent of U.S. respondents planned to work on green retrofits of existing buildings (the global average was 37 percent).

Demand for Construction Workers Around the World

The **recruitment firm** Michael Page recently conducted research to determine demand for specific careers by country. It found that there is a shortage of construction workers around the world. Here is a breakdown of popular construction careers and in which countries there is a shortage:

Builders: Australia, Germany, Russia, Switzerland

Carpenters: Australia, Canada, Norway

Construction Machine Operators: Canada, France, Sweden

Electricians: Australia, Canada, New Zealand, Norway, Russia

Glaziers: Australia, Canada, France, Switzerland

Plumbers: Australia, Canada, Germany, Norway, Russia, Switzerland

Roofers: Australia, Austria, Canada, Sweden

Stonemasons: Australia, Germany, Sweden, Switzerland

■ *The use of green construction techniques is becoming increasingly popular in both residential and commercial construction.*

Why Is Green Construction Becoming More Popular?

Builders surveyed by Dodge Data & Analytics and the National Association of Home Builders gave the following reasons for the increasing popularity of green building:

- Increasing customer demand
- Greater availability and affordability of green products
- The option to create a higher-quality home
- The rise in the value of green homes
- Financial incentives from government agencies or utilities
- Changes in building codes that make it easier to build green

In the United States, the highest percentage of respondents reported that they expected to "work on new green institutional projects (such as schools, hospitals and public buildings), green retrofits of existing buildings, and new green commercial construction (such as office and retail buildings)."

Home builders are also beginning to embrace green construction. One-third of single family home builders and multi-family home builders who were surveyed by Dodge Data & Analytics and the National Association of Home Builders (NAHB) in 2017 said that green building was at least 60 percent of their building operations. By 2022, this percentage should increase from 33 percent to 50 percent of builders. "Our members recognize the value of building green and are incorporating these elements into their standard business practices," according to Granger MacDonald, the chairman of the NAHB.

Challenges to Employment Growth

Green construction continues to grow in popularity, but some future developments may limit job growth in this building specialty area and the construction industry, in general. If the economy weakens and another recession occurs, the number of homes and other buildings that are under construction will decrease. Some people may choose not to spend money on the construction of green buildings, or purchase fewer green components (such as energy-efficient furnaces or solar panels). If this occurs, there will be less demand for green construction workers. On the other hand, green construction practices help people save money over the long term. If the public can be educated about this fact, many people may still hire green construction workers during a recession.

Could robots replace construction workers? Not yet, but maybe in the future—especially for large construction projects. Robots are rapidly replacing workers in many fields—especially manufacturing. The number of industrial robots being produced will grow to 521,000 by 2020, according to the International Federation of Robotics, an increase of 71 percent since 2016. In the construction industry, SAM, a brick-laying robot, is already working on job sites. SAM (an acronym for Semi-Automated-Mason), which was created by a company named Construction Robotics in 2015, can lay about eight hundred to twelve hundred bricks a day—as compared to the three hundred to five hundred bricks that a human mason can lay in the same amount of time. Additionally, scientists are developing robotic tiling machines that can install flooring, but none are in widespread use. Both these types of robots need programming and assistance from humans. And there are still tasks that can't be performed by robots. It's most likely that robotic construction "workers" will be used for large construction projects (factories, hospitals, sports stadiums, etc.) rather than in homes and other smaller construction projects because it would not be **cost-effective** to work in homes. As a result, construction workers will still be needed to work on home construction and repair, and other small jobs.

Green construction is a relatively new field, and employers report that there is still a shortage of construction workers who have green building skills. Job opportunities could decline if more people become experts in green construction. But since the field is still growing, it is unlikely that there will be a surplus of green construction workers in the near future.

In Closing

Do you care about protecting the environment? Do you like working with your hands? Do you like to solve problems as you build things? Would you like to earn good pay without a four-year degree? If you answered "yes" to all these questions, then a

Women in Green Construction

Women make up about 47 percent of the U.S. workforce, but only about 9 percent of workers in the construction industry, according to the U.S. Department of Labor. The percentage of women in green construction is unknown, but it is probably around 3 to 9 percent. Educational programs, construction associations, trade unions, government agencies, and others are trying to encourage more women to pursue careers in construction. The Women's Bureau of the U.S. Department of Labor reports that a career in green construction is especially attractive to women for the following reasons:

- Pay in green construction careers, which are dominated by men, is much higher than in traditionally female occupations.

- These careers can be entered by those with any skill level, and often provide good advancement opportunities.

- There are green construction jobs for almost any interest—from energy efficiency and building inspection, to carpentry, plumbing, and roofing.

- Many training paths (apprenticeships, college, on-the-job training, etc.) are available, which gives women from different economic backgrounds and family situations a variety of options to obtain the training they need to enter the field.

- Green jobs are personally satisfying to those who care about helping homeowners save money and reduce energy waste.

Here are a few organizations that support women in the construction industry:

- The Canadian Association of Women in Construction (http://www.cawic.ca) offers membership, a mentoring program, networking events, and a job bank at its website.

- The National Association of Home Builders (http://www.nahb.com) offers a Professional Women in Building group. Members receive *Building Women* magazine, networking opportunities, and the chance to apply for scholarships.

- The National Association of Women in Construction (NAWIC, http//www.nawic.org) offers membership, an annual meeting, and scholarships. It also publishes *The NAWIC IMAGE*.

rewarding career in green construction could be in your future. I hope that you'll use this book as a starting point to discover even more about careers in green construction. Talk to green building professionals about their careers and shadow them on the job, use the resources of professional organizations and unions, and try your hand at some green building practices to build your skills. Good luck exploring a career in green construction!

■ *Many career paths are available in green construction, including in solar power.*

Text-Dependent Questions

1. Can you name three reasons why employment prospects are good for green construction workers?

2. Why are careers in green construction such a good option for women?

3. What are some developments that might slow employment for green construction workers?

Research Project

Try to learn more about robotic tiling machines and SAM, the bricklaying robot. What tasks will they be able to perform, and which will still require humans? How will the introduction of robots change the work of green construction workers? Write a one-page report that summarizes your findings and present it in science class.

apprentice: A trainee who is enrolled in a program that prepares them to work as a skilled trades worker. Apprentices must complete 2,000 hours of on-the-job training and 144 hours of related classroom instruction during a four- to five-year course of study. They are paid a salary that increases as they obtain experience.

apprenticeship: A formal training program that often consists of 2,000 hours of on-the-job training and 144 hours of related classroom instruction per year for four to five years.

bid: A formal offer created by a contractor or trades worker that details the work that will be done, the amount the company or individual will charge, and the time frame in which the work will be completed.

blueprints: A reproduction of a technical plan for the construction of a home or other structure. Blueprints are created by licensed architects.

building codes: A series of rules established by local, state, regional, and national governments that ensure safe construction. The National Electrical Code, which was developed by the National Fire Protection Association, is an example of a building code in the United States.

building information modeling software: A computer application that uses a 3D model-based process that helps construction, architecture, and engineering professionals to more efficiently plan, design, build, and manage buildings and infrastructure.

building materials: Any naturally-occurring (clay, rocks, sand, wood, etc.) or human-made substances (steel, cement, etc.) that are used to construct buildings and other structures.

building permit: Written permission from a government entity that allows trades workers to construct, alter, or otherwise work at a construction site.

community college: A private or public two-year college that awards certificates and associate degrees.

general contractor: A licensed individual or company that accepts primary responsibility for work done at a construction site or in another setting.

green construction: The planning, design, construction, and operation of structures in an environmentally responsible manner. Green construction stresses energy and water efficiency, the use of eco-friendly construction materials (when possible), indoor environmental quality, and the structure's overall effects on its site or the larger community. Also known as **green building**.

inspection: The process of reviewing/examining ongoing or recently completed construction work to ensure that it has been completed per the applicable building codes. Construction and building inspectors are employed by government agencies and private companies that provide inspection services to potential purchasers of new construction or remodeled buildings.

job foreman: A journeyman (male or female) who manages a group of other journeymen and apprentices on a project.

journeyman: A trades worker who has completed an apprenticeship training. If licensed, he or she can work without direct supervision, but, for large projects, must work under permits issued to a master electrician.

Leadership in Energy and Environmental Design (LEED) certification: A third-party verification that remodeled or newly constructed buildings have met the highest criteria for water efficiency, energy efficiency, the use of eco-friendly materials and building practices, indoor environmental quality, and other criteria. LEED certification is the most popular green building rating system in the world.

master trades worker: A trades professional who has a minimum level of experience (usually at least three to four years as a licensed professional) and who has passed an examination. Master trades workers manage journeymen, trades workers, and apprentices.

prefabricated: The manufacture or fabrication of certain components of a structure (walls, electrical components, etc.) away from the construction site. Prefabricated products are brought to the construction site and joined with existing structures or components.

schematic diagram: An illustration of the components of a system that uses abstract, graphic symbols instead of realistic pictures or illustrations.

self-employment: Working for oneself as a small business owner, rather than for a corporation or other employer. Self-employed people are responsible for generating their own income, and they must provide their own fringe benefits (such as health insurance).

smart home technology: A system of interconnected devices that perform certain actions to save energy, time, and money.

technical college: A public or private college that offers two- or four-year programs in practical subjects, such as the trades, information technology, applied sciences, agriculture, and engineering.

union: An organization that seeks to gain better wages, benefits, and working conditions for its members. Also called a **labor union** or **trade union**.

zoning permit: A document issued by a government body that stipulates that the project in question meets existing zoning rules for a geographic area.

zoning rules: Restrictions established by government bodies as to what type of structure can be built in a certain area. For example, many cities have zoning rules that restrict the construction of factories in residential areas.

Index

Photo Credits

Further Reading & Internet Resources

Ching, Francis D. K., and Ian M. Shapiro. *Green Building Illustrated*. Hoboken, N.J.: John Wiley & Sons, 2014.

Cook, Miki, and Doug Garrett. *Green Home Building: Money-Saving Strategies for an Affordable, Healthy, High-Performance Home*. Gabriola Island, B.C., Canada: New Society Publishers, 2014.

Dykstra, Alison. *Green Construction: An Introduction to a Changing Industry*. San Francisco: Kirshner Publishing Company, 2016.

Kibert, Charles J. *Sustainable Construction: Green Building Design and Delivery*. 4th ed. Hoboken, N.J.: John Wiley & Sons, 2016.

Sweeney, James L. *Energy Efficiency: Building a Clean, Secure Economy*. Stanford, Calif.: Hoover Institution Press, 2016.

Wing, Charlie. *The Visual Handbook of Building and Remodeling*. Newtown, Conn.: The Taunton Press, 2018.

Internet Resources

https://www.bls.gov/green/construction. This website from the U.S. Department of Labor provides information on education and careers in green construction.

https://energy.gov/science-innovation/energy-efficiency. Visit this website to learn more about energy efficiency.

https://www.onetonline.org/find/green. This U.S. government website offers information on careers in green construction, energy efficiency, and other green economy sectors.

https://www.bls.gov/ooh/construction-and-extraction: This section of the *Occupational Outlook Handbook* features information on job duties, educational requirements, salaries, and the employment outlook for nearly twenty construction careers.

About the Author

Andrew Morkes has been a writer and editor for more than 25 years. He is the author of more than 20 books about college-planning and careers, including many titles in this series, the *Vault Career Guide to Social Media*, and *They Teach That in College!?: A Resource Guide to More Than 100 Interesting College Majors*, which was selected as one of the best books of the year by the library journal *Voice of Youth Advocates*. He is also the author and publisher of "The Morkes Report: College and Career Planning Trends" blog.

Video Credits

Chapter 1: Learn more about green building and the Leadership in Energy and Environmental Design green rating system: http://x-qr.net/1G7e

Learn how green construction techniques have been implemented at the National Renewable Energy Laboratory's Research Support Facility to save energy and money: http://x-qr.net/1Eb0

Chapter 2: Follow a day in the life of a solar installer: http://x-qr.net/1Gfk

Learn more about how masonry is used in sustainable building: http://x-qr.net/1F6q

Chapter 4: Learn about a green construction training program: http://x-qr.net/1GJb

Chapter 5: A high school student builds a tiny house from the ground up: http://x-qr.net/1GHh

Chapter 6: Learn why so many people are embracing green building: http://x-qr.net/1H26